Government

Our Government and Citizenship

SPIRIT
of America®

Government

HOW LOCAL, STATE, AND FEDERAL GOVERNMENT WORKS

By Mark Friedman

Content Adviser: David R. Smith, PhD, Academic Advisor and Adjunct
Assistant Professor of History, The University of Michigan, Ann Arbor, Michigan

The Child's World
Chanhassen, Minnesota

Government

Published in the United States of America by The Child's World®
PO Box 326 • Chanhassen, MN 55317-0326 • 800-599-READ • www.childsworld.com

Acknowledgments
The Child's World®: Mary Berendes, Publishing Director

Editorial Directions, Inc.: E. Russell Primm, Editorial Director; Pam Rosenberg, Line Editor; Katie
Marsico, Associate Editor; Judi Shiffer, Associate Editor and Library Media Specialist; Matthew
Messbarger, Editorial Assistant; Susan Hindman, Copy Editor; Lucia Raatma, Proofreader; Judith
Frisbee, Peter Garnham, and Olivia Nellums, Fact Checkers; Tim Griffin/IndexServ, Indexer; Cian
Loughlin O'Day, Photo Researcher; Linda S. Koutris, Photo Selector

Photo
Cover: Interior photographs: Cover/frontispiece: Joseph Sohm; ChromoSohm Inc./Corbis.
Interior: AP/Wide World: 11 (Al Goldis), 14, 18 (Staci E. McKee), 24 (William Wilson Lewis, III),
25 (Jerome T. Nakagawa/File); Bettmann/Corbis: 7, 15; Corbis: 6 (Paul Colangelo), 9 (Joseph Sohm;
ChromoSohm Inc.), 10 (Richard T. Nowitz), 16 (Michael S. Lewis), 19 (Phil Schermeister), 21 (Ken
James), 22 (Ted Streshinsky), 23 (Ted Horowitz), 26 (Owen Franken), 27 (James Leynse), 28 (Jason
Reed/Reuters); Getty Images: 8 (Hulton|Archive), 13 (David Hume Kennerly), 17 (Phil Mislinski),
20 (Erik Hill).

Registration
The Child's World®, Spirit of America®, and their associated logos are the sole property and
registered trademarks of The Child's World®.

Library of Congress Cataloging-in-Publication Data
Friedman, Mark, 1963–
  Government : how local, state, and federal government works / by Mark Friedman.
    p. cm. — (Our government and citizenship)
  Includes index.
  ISBN 1-59296-323-4 (library bound : alk. paper) 1. United States—Politics and government—
Juvenile literature. I. Title. II. Series.
  JK40.F75 2005
  320.473—dc22   2004007201

14 19 24

Contents

Chapter ONE

Separate Powers, Separate Governments

St. Augustine, Florida, is the oldest city in the United States. The mayor and other local government officials work in the St. Augustine City Hall building.

WHEN YOU TALK ABOUT "THE GOVERNMENT," DO you ever think about *which* government you mean? No matter where you live in the United States, you are served by three or more different governments: the national government, the government of your state, and the government of the town, city, county, or other **municipality** in which you live. These national, state, and local governments work together and separately—and that's exactly the way the nation was designed to work more than two centuries ago.

In 1781, the United States set up its first national government under rules spelled out in the **Articles of Confederation.** Under these rules, states tended

6

Discontented citizens seize a courthouse during Shay's Rebellion, a revolt against economic conditions and high taxes led by some citizens of western Massachusetts. The rebellion began in 1786 and was one event that helped convince colonial leaders that the United States needed a strong national government.

to act more like different countries than like parts of the same country. The national government was not strong enough to organize the states and force them to do what was in the best interest of the nation as a whole. For example, the government couldn't organize a unified army to defend the country.

In May 1787, a convention was held in Philadelphia, Pennsylvania, the nation's capital at the time. Representatives from every state were invited to this meeting to write a new set of rules for the government. They discussed the issues, argued about solutions, and finally reached

Interesting Fact

▶ The city of Philadelphia served as the capital of the United States until 1800. In October of that year, Washington, D.C., became the nation's capital. President John Adams moved into the new White House and Congress met for the first time in the new Capitol.

a compromise. Four months later, the United States Constitution was approved by the delegates.

One thing the delegates agreed on from the start of the **Constitutional Convention** was this: The nation's government needed more power, but its power must be held in check. The delegates feared that if any part of government had too much power, citizens would lose their freedoms. Nobody wanted a government that would rule over the people. They wanted a government that would assist people and defend their rights.

How could they create a government that was powerful enough to organize all the states, but wasn't *too* powerful? The authors of the

George Washington leads the discussion at the Constitutional Convention in 1787.

The U.S. Constitution was drafted at this desk in Independence Hall.

Constitution solved this puzzle with the idea of separation of powers—giving different responsibilities to different parts of government. Some powers would belong to the president, others to members of the **legislature,** and still others to the courts.

In addition, the national government would have power in certain areas, while other powers would be reserved for smaller state and local governments that are closer to the people. This distribution of powers between the national and state governments is known as federalism. The strong national government became known as the federal government.

Imagine what life might be like without a strong federal government. There would be problems in many parts of everyday life. For instance, it makes sense for everyone in the nation to use the same kind of money. If each state made its own money, it would be too difficult to do business as one nation. So under the U.S. Constitution, only the national government has the power to print (or coin) money—the states are not allowed to do so.

This sheet of $100 bills was printed by the federal government. The bills will be cut apart and put into circulation. They can be spent anywhere in the United States.

Decisions about how children should be taught and how schools should be run are left up to state and local governments.

It also makes sense for the national government to decide if the nation should go to war against other countries. This means that even if your state is extremely angry with another state or country, it is not allowed to form its own army and go to war. The same kinds of rules apply to the local governments of your town or city—they can't declare war either.

At the same time, there are many responsibilities the Constitution gives to state and local governments that the national government does not have. One example is providing education for children. If you go to a public school, it gets its money from, and is run by, your local and state governments, not by the national government in Washington, D.C.

The National Government

THERE ARE THREE BRANCHES OF THE FEDERAL GOVernment, each charged with different responsibilities. The legislative branch (the House of Representatives and the Senate) creates laws for the nation. The executive branch (headed by the president of the United States) executes, or carries out, the laws. The judicial branch (the Supreme Court and other lower courts) interprets the laws and can overrule them.

In addition to separating powers, the Constitution also provides for numerous ways in which these bodies of government overlap. This is so they can check up on one another in case one body does something that isn't good for the country.

The president of the United States proposes a **budget** for the national government, but Congress must approve the president's budget. Congress can create new laws, but the president can **veto** a law before it goes into effect. The president can recommend new justices for the U.S. Supreme Court, but the Senate must approve those people before they can join the court.

These are just a few examples of the many ways in which the three branches check one another's work. Because they can do so, the power among the branches remains equal, or balanced. This system of checks and balances is another key idea written into the Constitution.

For a long time during the Constitutional Convention, delegates disagreed about how Congress should be set up. The small states argued that each state should send the same number of representatives

Supreme Court justice Sandra Day O'Connor takes an oath during her Senate confirmation hearings in 1981. The president can nominate a new Supreme Court justice, but the Senate must approve that nomination.

Roger Sherman was one of the Connecticut delegates to the Constitution Convention. He was born in 1721 in Massachusetts. He served as a member of the U.S. House of Representatives and as a U.S. Senator under the constitution he helped to create.

Interesting Fact

▶ There are seven states that have only one representative in the U.S. House of Representatives: Alaska, Delaware, Montana, North Dakota, South Dakota, Vermont, and Wyoming. The state with the largest number of representatives is California with 53 members.

to Congress. The big states said that states with large populations should be able to send more representatives than smaller states. After months of debate, two Connecticut delegates, Roger Sherman and Oliver Ellsworth, came up with a solution that came to be known as the Great Compromise. They proposed two bodies of Congress—the House of Representatives and the Senate.

This arrangement creates a **bicameral** legislature. To this day, states send different numbers of representatives to the House (based on the size of the state's population), and every state sends just two representatives (senators) to the Senate.

THE MOST IMPORTANT BUSINESS OF CONGRESS IS TO MAKE NEW LAWS. EVERY law starts out as a **bill.** Once a representative introduces a bill, it is examined by a group, or committee, of members of Congress. After the committee has finished its research, it can either approve the bill, approve it with changes, or decide it's no good and "kill" it.

If the bill is still alive, it is brought to the floor of the House or Senate. First, one group discusses it, suggests changes or additions if needed, and then votes on it. If the majority of votes are in favor, the bill is then sent to the other Congressional body. There, it is examined and voted on again.

In the end, if both the House and Senate approve a bill, it becomes a law—but only if it survives one important, final checkpoint. The president of the United States must approve the bill. If the president signs the bill, it is approved and becomes a law. If the president thinks the bill is wrong or has major problems in the way it is written, the bill is vetoed, or rejected.

There are ways of overcoming a veto. If the president explains what is wrong with the bill, Congress can change those things and the bill becomes law. Or, if two-thirds of the members of Congress disagree with the president and favor the bill, they can **override** the president's veto.

Chapter THREE

State Governments

The Montana State Capitol is located in Helena, Montana.

STATE GOVERNMENTS ARE BUILT MUCH LIKE THE federal government. Each state has its own constitution, which spells out how the executive, legislative, and judicial branches work together.

State constitutions call for the separation of powers and create checks and balances. This ensures that their governments will act fairly and properly.

The people in a state vote to elect a governor to head the executive branch. Governors carry out the laws of the state. They oversee many departments that handle the money, education, roads, public safety, and welfare of the state's citizens.

All state judicial branches include a state supreme court—the highest court in the state. Below it is a system of lower courts, which make decisions

Interesting Fact

▶ Eight states wrote their original state constitutions in 1776—Delaware, Maryland, New Hampshire, New Jersey, North Carolina, Pennsylvania, South Carolina, and Virginia.

Members of Nebraska's senate work in the Senate chambers. Nebraska had a bicameral state legislature until 1934 when citizens voted to do away with the state's House of Representatives.

Interesting Fact

▶ There are currently 49 senators in the Nebraska Legislature. Senators are elected to four-year terms. They are paid $12,000 per year for their legislative work, so most of them have other full-time jobs.

on legal cases involving people, companies, or government agencies that are in disagreement with one another.

Like the U.S. Congress, almost every state legislature is a bicameral body. Nebraska is the exception: it has a unicameral (one house) legislature—only a Senate.

States have different names for their legislatures. Some use the name General Assembly, others use Legislative Assembly, and two states (Massachusetts and New Hampshire) call their legislatures the General Court. One thing all states have in common is that these houses of government are staffed by elected officials who represent districts throughout the state.

Like the federal legislative branch, state legislatures create laws. But state laws concern only the

18

state and its citizens. State laws cannot conflict with any law or principle in the constitutions of other states or the nation. Nor can they go against other federal law.

So why do states need their own individual laws? The United States is a huge country, and every state is different in countless ways. States have different geography—some have many bodies of water, some are rich with forests, some contain deserts, and some feature mountain ranges. So laws about how people and businesses use their land and water must be different from state to state. For instance, a state such as Arizona—with a lot of desert and few sources of water—needs laws regarding water usage and conservation. A state with plentiful sources of water, such as Minnesota, does not need the same laws.

The state of Minnesota has many lakes. Its government officials may need to enact laws to make sure that people keep the lakes clean.

Fishing is an important industry in Alaska. Its state legislators must work to balance the interests of fishers with the need to protect the state's natural resources.

States also have different businesses and industries. Kansas has many farms that produce wheat and beef cattle, so there are state laws that regulate how those farms do business. But there aren't many fish farms in Kansas, so the state would have little use for Alaska's many laws concerning its large fishing industry.

States have different histories and cultures. In Illinois, for instance, the Polish-American Revolutionary War hero Casmir Pulaski is honored with a state holiday. This is because Chicago, Illinois, has the largest Polish-American population in the country. This holiday wouldn't make as much sense in a state with a smaller Polish population.

ONE OF THE MOST IMPORTANT RESPONSIBILITIES OF GOVERNMENT IS managing money. Every year, in both national and state governments, the executive branch creates a budget that the legislative branch must approve.

In each state, the head of each department lets the governor know how much money that department needs. For instance, the person in charge of the state police might tell the governor that money is needed for 10 new police cars. The library department requests money to supply public libraries across the state with new books and Internet access, and to hire and train library staff.

As chief executive, the governor has to figure out where the state will get the money to pay for these and other services. Most states have an income tax, which takes part of each working citizen's pay and sends it to the government. Many states also have a sales tax, which means that the government gets a fee for every item sold in stores or online in the state.

The governor's biggest challenge is coming up with a balanced budget— one in which the state spends no more than it collects in taxes. This is where the governor has to make tough choices. If the state doesn't have enough money, the governor may have to cut certain programs out of the budget. Or the governor may have to suggest raising tax rates or creating brand-new taxes. A governor gathers information and gets advice from legislators and others to try to make decisions that are best for the state and its citizens.

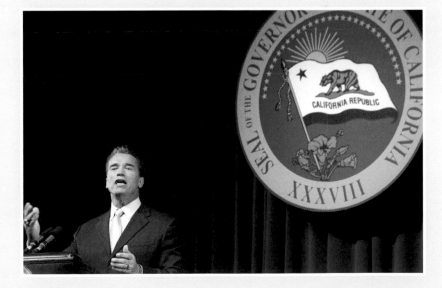

Chapter FOUR

Local Governments

Local government officials are responsible for making decisions about which streets need repairs in their town.

LIKE FEDERAL AND STATE GOVERNMENTS, LOCAL governments pass and enforce laws, create budgets, and have courts. But they work on much smaller details than state or national governments.

Who decides where to install traffic lights or paint crosswalks in your town center? Who decides the schedule for trash and recycling pickup in your neighborhood? Who hires the firefighters and purchases their vehicles and equipment? Who runs your park district and builds public playgrounds?

All of these tasks, and many more, are the work of local governments. They are called local governments because they employ people who live and work in the

community. They understand issues locally, or close to home.

It would be silly for the federal government in Washington, D.C., or even your state government, to do the local government's work. For instance, how could a big government hundreds of miles away know enough about your elementary school to make decisions such as who to hire as principal or how many students should be in each class? These are important decisions but are best made by people who are in the community every day. So citizens elect a school board—a local government body to run the public schools in one town or a group of towns.

Decisions that affect local safety, such as hiring firefighters and providing them with the equipment they need, are left up to local governments.

Local governments come in many different shapes and sizes. All states except Louisiana and Alaska are broken up into regions called counties. In Louisiana these regions are called parishes and in Alaska they are known as boroughs. Each county, parish, or borough contains several different cities, towns, or villages. The county government oversees services that these communities share.

Some regional and city governments are huge. California's Los Angeles County government runs the largest county in the nation. It contains more than 100 towns and cities, including the city of Los Angeles. With about 10 million residents,

A citizen speaks at a school board meeting in Riverside, California.

Los Angeles County has a larger population than most states, so its government needs to be very large to serve all those people. Still, it is a local government.

The smallest county in the country is Loving County, Texas. It has a population of only 70. The county government there employs less than a dozen people, and some of those people have more than one job. In 2004, one person served as sheriff and tax assessor for Loving County.

Many city and town governments are set up with a separation of powers similar to the federal government. The people elect a mayor to run the executive branch, and the legislative branch is headed by a city or town council. These representatives come from different neighborhoods, or districts.

The city of Los Angeles is part of the largest county in the United States.

The city council of Asheville, North Carolina, meets.

This is not the only way to run local governments, however. Many municipalities choose not to have a separation of powers. They elect a council, and the council hires a city manager, who is in charge of running all the different city departments.

As citizens, it is up to all of us to help make sure that our federal, state, and local governments work the way the founders of our country intended. That is why it is important for all of us to make our voices heard. When you are old enough to vote, make sure to register and vote for the people who

26

best represent your interests. Then, when those people are in office, take the time to share your opinions with them. That is the only way we will truly have what Abraham Lincoln called "government of the people, by the people, and for the people."

A woman registers to vote in New York City. Voting is an important way to make your opinions known.

THE EXECUTIVE AND LEGISLATIVE BRANCHES OF GOVERNMENT ARE MOSTLY concerned with setting up and carrying out laws and budgets, and providing services for citizens. The judicial branch comes into play when problems arise. If a person is accused of breaking a law or harming others, a court will judge and possibly punish that person. That is a key responsibility of the judicial branch.

In a court, there is always a judge. Depending on the type of case, there may be a jury. If a judge or a jury decides that a person is guilty of a crime, that person can appeal the decision. This means taking the same case to a higher court to be argued again, before a different judge (and jury, if necessary). The final court of appeals in a state is the state supreme court. If the U.S. Supreme Court in Washington, D.C., agrees to hear the case, its decision is the final word on the matter.

In any supreme court, a panel of justices hears the cases. There are no juries. The head of the U.S. Supreme Court is called the chief justice. In many cases that reach supreme courts, a person is trying to prove that he

or she is innocent of wrongdoing because the *law* is wrong. Only supreme courts have the power to decide whether or not a law is **unconstitutional.** This is the key checks-and-balances function of the judicial branch of government: If laws are wrong or unjust, there is a way to have them changed.

1775 The Revolutionary War begins.

1776 The Declaration of Independence is approved by the American colonists.

1781 The Articles of Confederation are ratified, setting up the first U.S. national government.

1783 The Revolutionary War ends.

1787 The Constitutional Convention is held in Philadelphia, Pennsylvania, from May to September.

1788 The U.S. Constitution takes effect.

1789 The Supreme Court is created; George Washington becomes the first president of the United States.

1791 The Bill of Rights is approved.

1793 The federal government establishes a mint in Philadelphia, Pennsylvania, to create coins that can be used throughout the nation.

1800 The federal government moves to its new home in Washington, D.C.

1801 Thomas Jefferson of Virginia is the first state governor to become U.S. president.

1825 John Quincy Adams is the first son of a former U.S. president to hold the same office as his father. (In 2000, George W. Bush would become the second.)

1870 Mississippi senator Hiram R. Revels and South Carolina congressman Joseph H. Rainey become the first African-American members of the U.S. Congress.

1916 Jeannette Rankin of Montana becomes the first woman elected to the U.S. Congress.

1925 Nellie Tayloe Ross of Wyoming becomes the first woman to serve as the governor of a state.

1945 President Franklin Delano Roosevelt dies after 12 years in office, the longest term of any U.S. president.

1961 Thurgood Marshall becomes the first African-American to serve on the U.S. Supreme Court.

1974 Richard M. Nixon becomes the first U.S. president to resign from office.

1981 Sandra Day O'Connor becomes the first woman to serve on the U.S. Supreme Court.

Articles of Confederation (AR-tih-kuhls UV kon-fed-uh-RAY-shun)
The Articles of Confederation was the first document setting up the government of the United States. In 1788, the U.S. Constitution replaced the Articles of Confederation.

bicameral (bi-KAM-ruhl)
If a legislature is bicameral, it is made of up two different legislative bodies. The U.S. Congress is an example of a bicameral legislature because it is made up of the Senate and the House of Representatives.

bill (BILL)
A bill is a written idea for a new law that is going to be debated by a legislature. Every law starts out as a bill.

budget (BUHJ-it)
A budget is a plan for how a person or organization will earn and spend money. Congress must approve the president's budget.

Constitutional Convention (kon-stih-TOO-shuhn-uhl kuhn-VEN-shuhn)
The Constitutional Convention was the meeting held in 1787 at which delegates created the U.S. Constitution. The Constitutional Convention was held in Philadelphia, Pennsylvania.

legislature (LEJ-iss-lay-chur)
A legislature is a body of government that has the power to make laws for a state or country.

municipality (myu-nis-uh-PAL-uh-tee)
A municipality is a political unit that sets up its own government. No matter where you live in the United States, you are served by three or more different governments—the national government, the government of your state, and the government of the town, city, county, or other municipality in which you live.

override (oh-vuhr-RIDE)
To override a veto means to set it aside. If two-thirds of the members of Congress disagree with the president and favor a bill that has been vetoed, they can override the president's veto.

unconstitutional (un-kon-stuh-TOO-shuhn-uhl)
Something that is unconstitutional goes against the laws set up by the constitution of a country or state. Only supreme courts have the power to decide whether or not a law is unconstitutional.

veto (VEE-toe)
To veto something means to refuse to approve it. Congress can create new laws, but the president can veto a law before it goes into effect.

For Further INFORMATION

Web Sites

Visit our home page for lots of links about federal, state, and local government:
http://www.childsworld.com/links.html

Note to Parents, Teachers, and Librarians:
We routinely verify our Web links to make sure they're safe,
active sites—so encourage your readers to check them out!

Books

Giesecke, Ernestine. *State Government.* Chicago: Heinemann Library, 2000.

Kowalski, Kathiann M. *A Balancing Act: A Look at Checks and Balances.*
Minneapolis: Lerner Publications, 2004.

Landau, Elaine. *The President's Work: A Look at the Executive Branch.* Minneapolis:
Lerner Publications, 2004.

Weidner, Daniel. *Creating the Constitution: The People and Events That Formed
the Nation.* Berkeley Heights, N.J.: Enslow Publishers, 2002.

Places to Visit or Contact

The National Archives Building
To see the U.S. Constitution and learn more about this important document
700 Pennsylvania Avenue NW
Washington, DC 20408
866/272-6272

The White House
To write for more information about the executive branch of government
1600 Pennsylvania Avenue NW
Washington, DC 20500

Index

About the Author

MARK FRIEDMAN IS A CHILDREN'S AUTHOR AND EDITOR WHO LIVES in Deerfield, Illinois, with his wife and daughter. He has written nonfiction children's books about countries, cities, and holidays, as well as several early readers. He has also edited hundreds of nonfiction books for readers of all ages.